AdvanceTime®

O

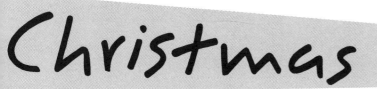

Christmas

**Arranged
by
Faber
& Faber**

___

Level 5

Pianistic Arrangements for
the Advancing Pianist

Production: Frank and Gail Hackinson
Production Coordinator: Marilyn Cole
Music Editor: Edwin McLean
Cover: Terpstra Design, San Francisco
Engraving: Graybear Music Company, Hollywood, Florida

FABER
PIANO ADVENTURES®
3042 Creek Drive
Ann Arbor, Michigan 48108

A NOTE TO TEACHERS

AdvanceTime® Piano Level 5 Christmas is a collection of Christmas and winter holiday favorites arranged for the advancing pianist. These imaginative and pianistic arrangements offer a variety of sounds and moods, always capturing the spirit of the Christmas season.

Teachers will find ample opportunity for the student to work on arpeggios, scales, 2-hand gestures, balance between the hands, balance within the hand, chord voicing, and octave playing—all within a delightful musical context.

AdvanceTime® Piano Level 5 is the level which follows *BigTime® Piano* (level 4 of the *PreTime®* to *BigTime® Piano Supplementary Library* arranged by Faber & Faber). It is written for the late intermediate pianist. A student at this level might also be studying a Kuhlau sonatina or a Bach 2-part invention.

Following are the levels of the *PreTime®* to *BigTime® Piano Supplementary Library,* which prepare the pianist for *AdvanceTime® Piano.*

PreTime® Piano	(Primer Level)
PlayTime® Piano	(Level 1)
ShowTime® Piano	(Level 2A)
ChordTime® Piano	(Level 2B)
FunTime® Piano	(Level 3A–3B)
BigTime® Piano	(Level 4)

Each level offers books in a variety of styles, making it possible for the teacher to offer stimulating material for every student. For a complimentary detailed listing, e-mail faber@pianoadventures.com or write us at the mailing address below.

Visit **www.PianoAdventures.com.**

ISBN 978-1-61677-124-9

TABLE OF CONTENTS

Silent Night

Words by
JOSEPH MOHR

Music by
FRANZ GRÜBER

Jingle Bells

Words and Music by
J. PIERPONT

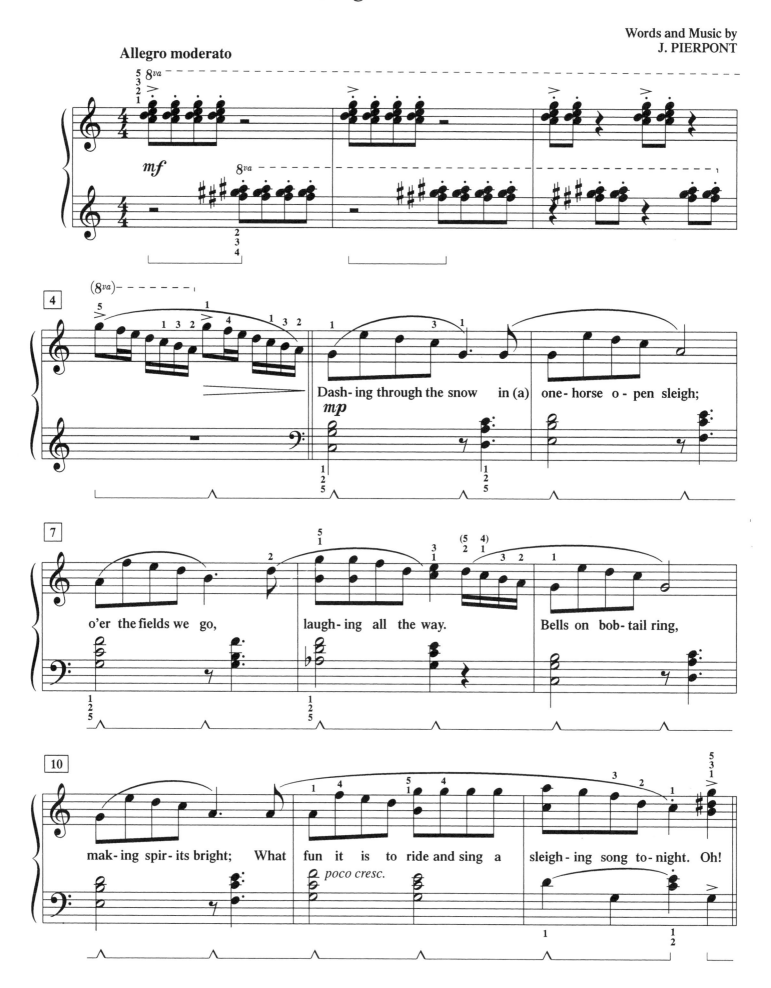

FF1124

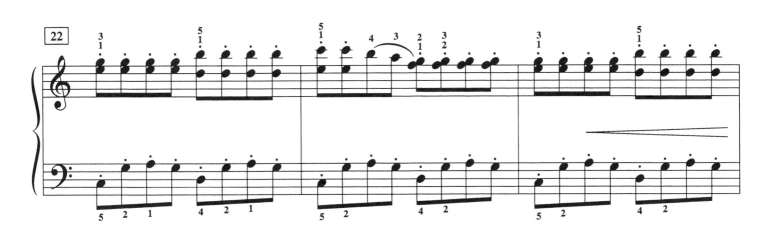

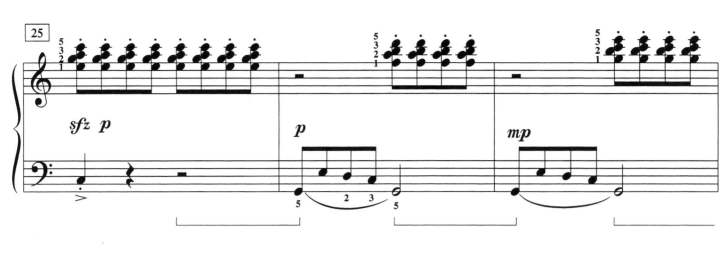

Go, Tell It on the Mountain

Traditional

sempre staccato

Over the River and Through the Woods

Traditional American

Lively and playfully (♩. = 69-80)

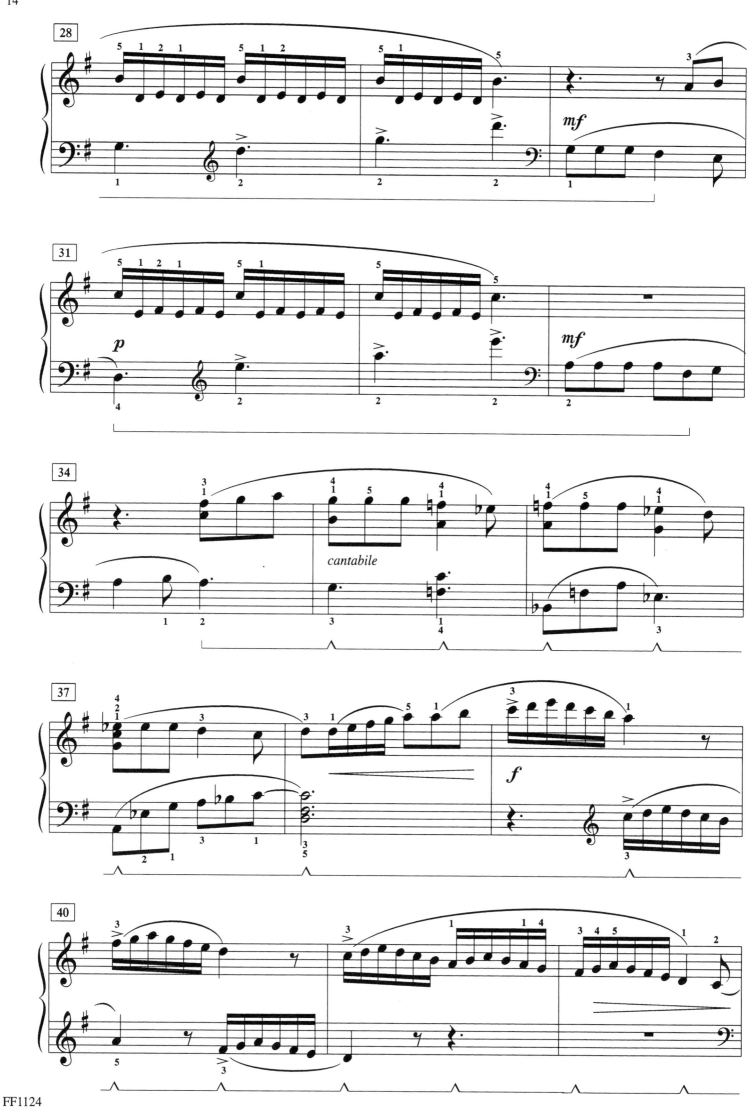

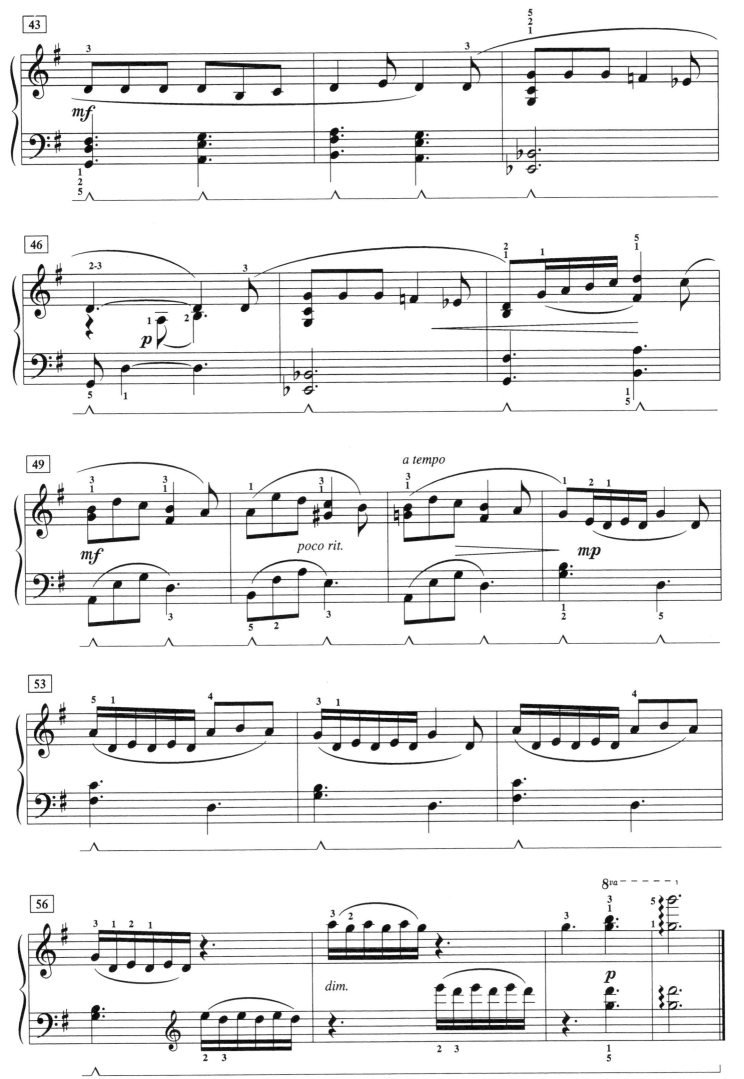

We Wish You a Merry Christmas

Traditional English Carol

tid - ings   for   Christ - mas   and   a   hap - py   New   Year!

Skaters' Waltz

Emile Charles Waldteufel

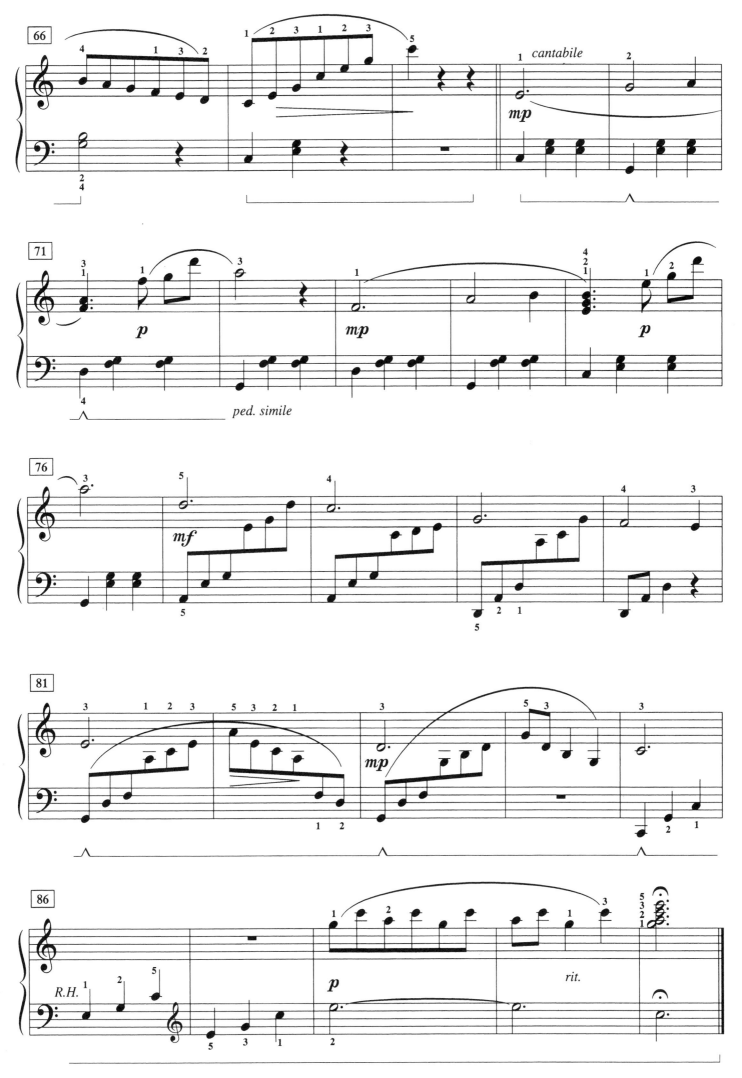

Auld Lang Syne

Traditional

God Rest Ye Merry, Gentlemen

Traditional

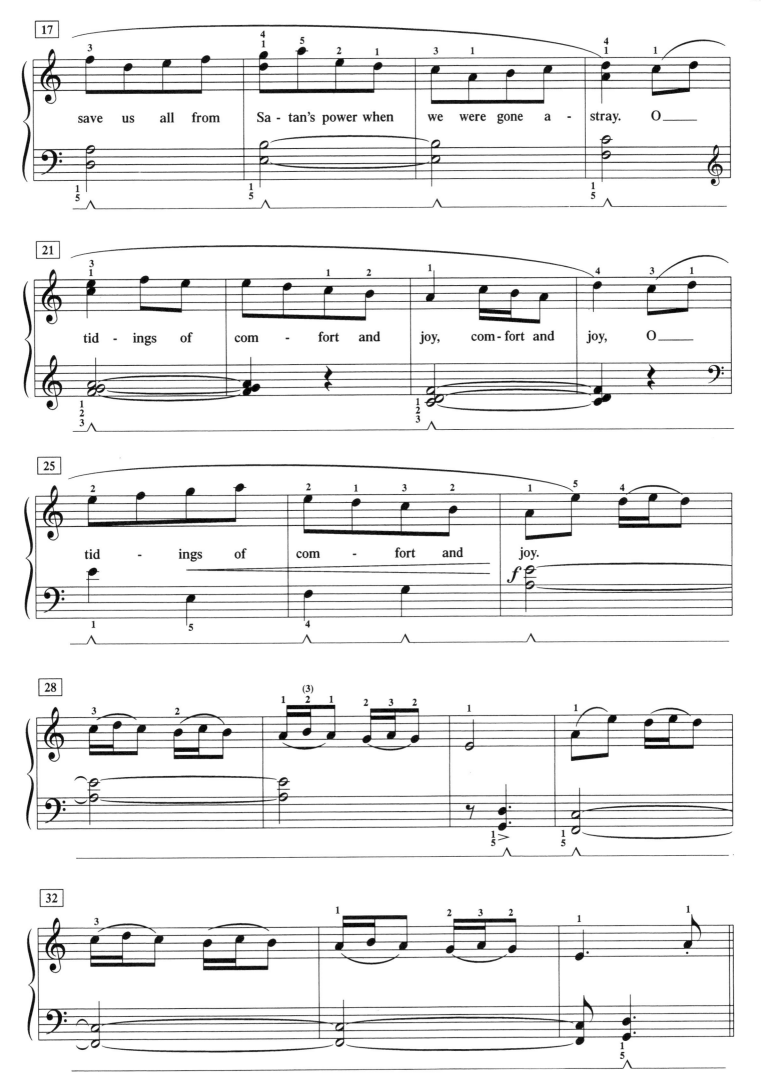

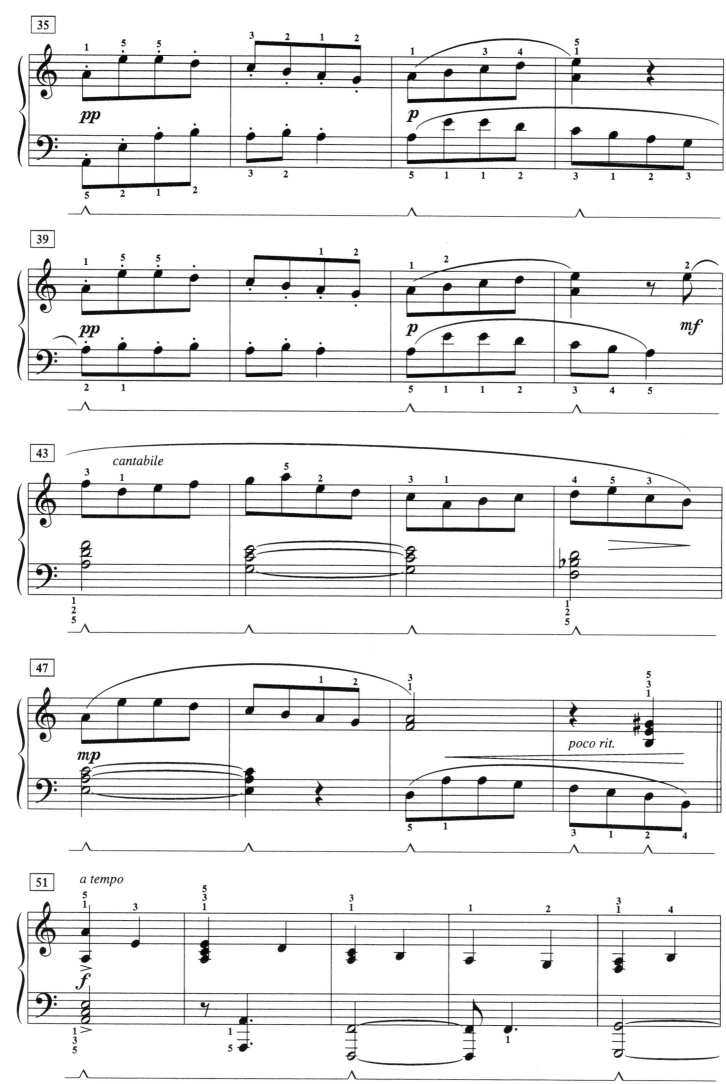

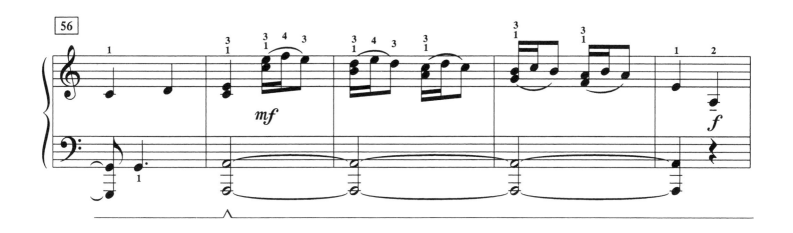

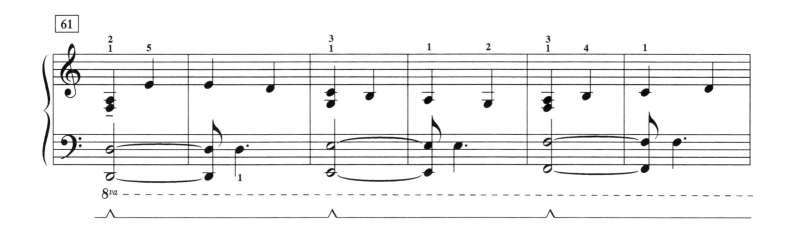

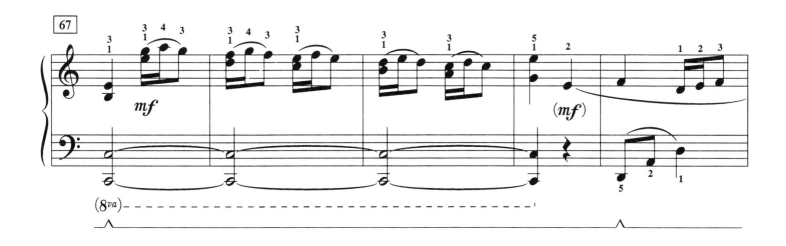

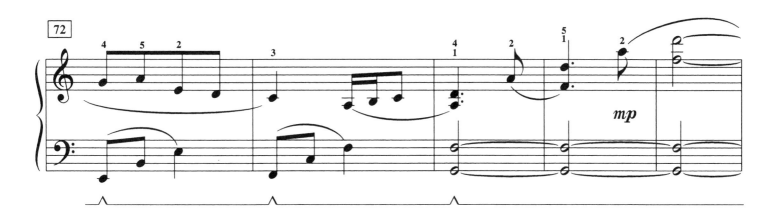

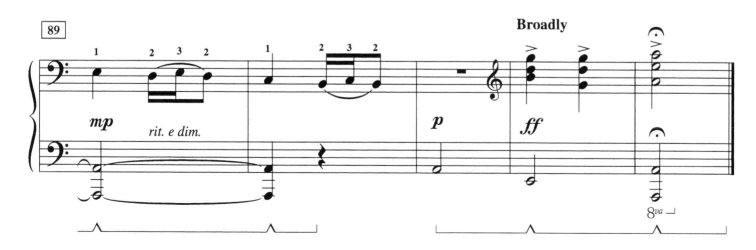

March
(from *The Nutcracker Suite*, Op. 71)

Peter Ilyich Tchaikovsky

FF1124

30

FF1124

Dance of the Reed Pipes
(from *The Nutcracker Suite*, Op. 71)

Peter Ilyich Tchaikovsky

A Celebration of Carols
(A Christmas Medley)

O Little Town of Bethlehem
L. Redner

O lit - tle town of Beth - le - hem, how

still we see thee lie. A -

We Three Kings of Orient Are
J. H. Hopkins, Jr.

Moving gracefully (♩ = 132)

We three kings of
Or - i - ent are; bear - ing gifts we tra - verse a-

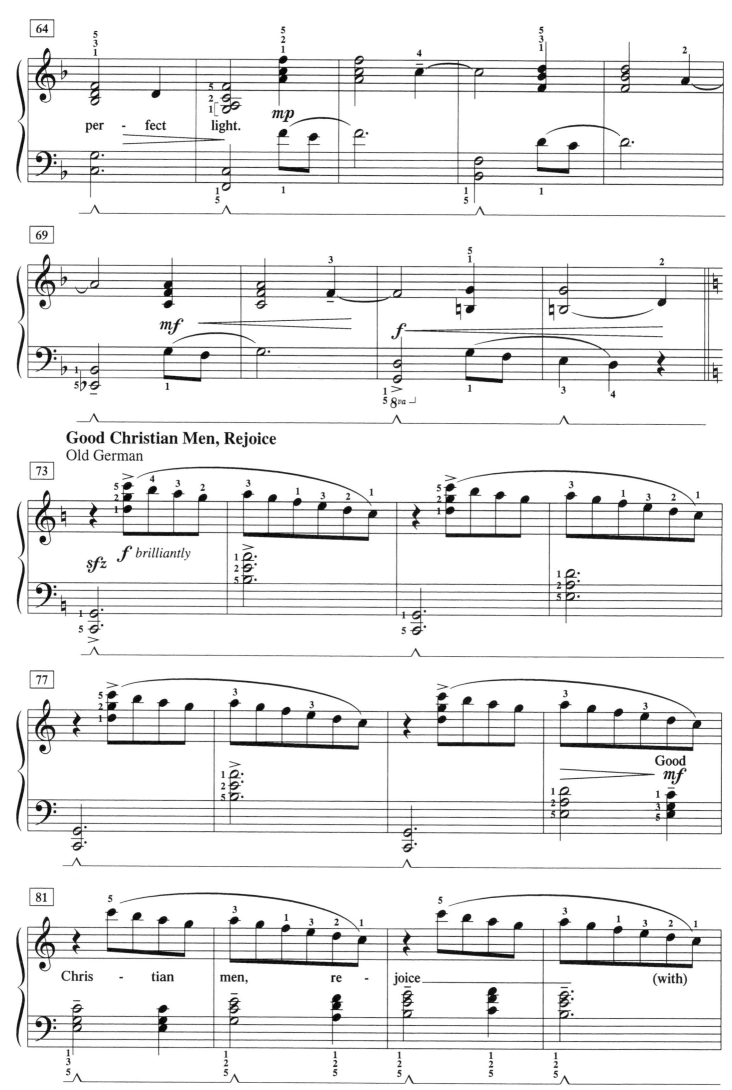

Good Christian Men, Rejoice

Old German

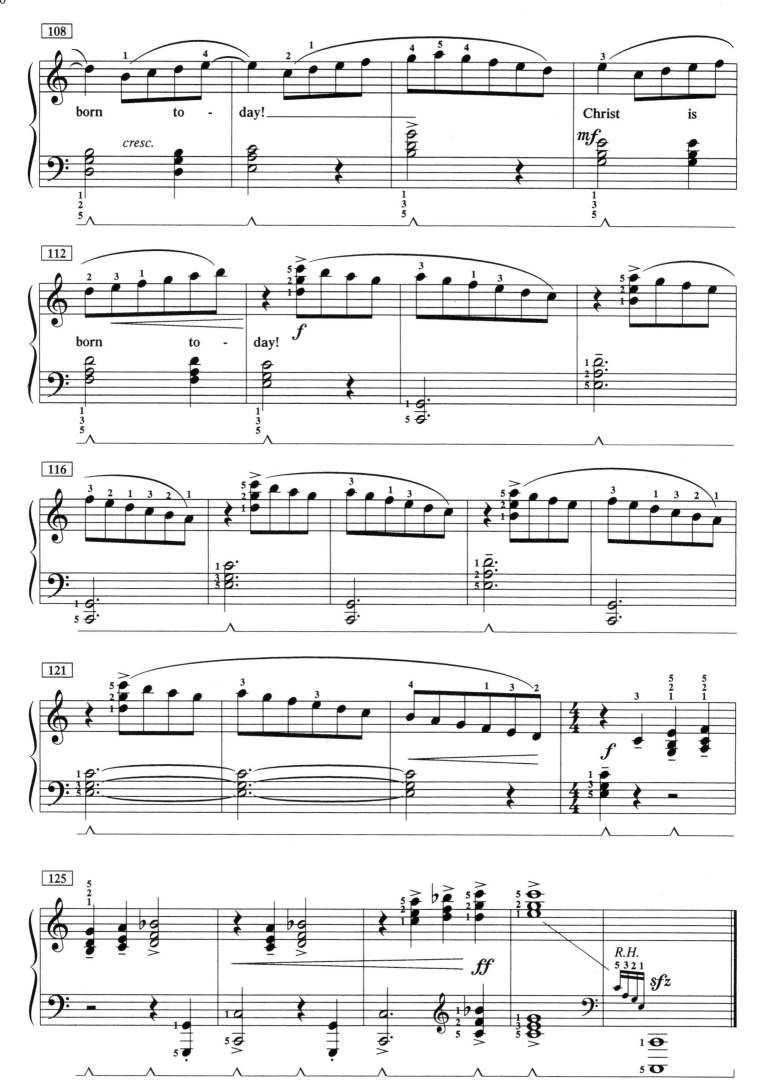